■SCHOLASTIC

Writing Lessons to Meet the Common Core

Grade 2

Linda Ward Beech

NEW YORK ● TORONTO ● LONDON ● AUCKLAND ● SYDNEY
MEXICO CITY ● NEW DELHI ● HONG KONG ● BUENOS AIRES

Teaching Resources

Cover design by Scott Davis
Interior design by Kathy Massaro
Illustrations by Maxie Chambliss, Rusty Fletcher, Anne Kennedy, and Bari Weissman

ISBN: 978-0-545-49598-1

2   3   4   5   6   7   8   9   10   40   20   19   18   17   16   15   14   13

Contents

About This Book

. . . .

To build a foundation for college and career readiness, students need to learn to use writing as a way of offering and supporting opinions, demonstrating understanding of the subjects they are studying, and conveying real and imagined experiences and events. They learn to appreciate that a key purpose of writing is to communicate clearly to an external, sometimes unfamiliar audience, and they begin to adapt the form and content of their writing to accomplish a particular task and purpose.

—COMMON CORE STATE STANDARDS FOR ENGLISH LANGUAGE ARTS, JUNE 2010

Support for Second Graders

. . . .

The first lesson in each section focuses on an important skill—fact and opinion for opinion writing, main idea for informative writing, and sequence for narrative writing. These introductory lessons provide the scaffolding students need to be successful in each of these writing forms.

This book includes step-by-step instructions for teaching the three forms of writing—Opinion, Informative/Explanatory, and Narrative—covered in the Common Core State Standards (CCSS). The CCSS are a result of a state-led effort to establish a single set of clear educational standards aimed at providing students nationwide with a high-quality education. The standards outline the knowledge and skills that students should achieve during their years in school.

The writing standards are a subset of the Common Core English Language Arts Standards. They provide "a focus for instruction" to help students gain a mastery of a range of skills and applications necessary for writing clear prose. This book is divided into three main sections; each section includes six lessons devoted to one of the writing forms covered in the CCSS for grade 2. You'll find more about each of these types of writing on pages 6–7.

- **Lessons 1–6** (pages 8–25) focus on the standards for writing opinion pieces.
- **Lessons 7–12** (pages 26–43) emphasize standards particular to informative/explanatory writing.
- **Lessons 13–18** (pages 44–61) address the standards for narrative writing.

Although the CCSS do not specify how to teach any form of writing, the lessons in this book follow the gradual release of responsibility model of instruction: I Do It, We Do It, You Do It (Pearson & Gallagher, 1983). This model provides educators with a framework for releasing responsibility to students in a gradual manner. It recognizes that we learn best when a concept is demonstrated to us; when we have sufficient time to practice it with support; and when we are then given the opportunity to try it on our own. Each phase is equally important, but the chief goal is to teach for independence—the You Do It phase—so that students really learn to take over the skill and apply it in new situations.

Pearson, P. D., & Gallagher, M. C. (1983). "The Instruction of Reading Comprehension." *Contemporary Educational Psychology*, 8 (3).

A Look at the Lessons

The lessons in each section progress in difficulty and increase in the number of objectives and standards covered. This format enables you to use beginning or later lessons in a section depending on your students' abilities. Each lesson includes a list of the objectives and standards included. A general reproducible offering students an assessment checklist of standards for each writing form appears at the end of the book. (See pages 62–64.)

Here's a look at the features in each lesson.

Lesson Page 1

The first page is the teaching page of each lesson. It provides a step-by-step plan for using the student reproducible on the second lesson page and the On Your Own activity on the third lesson page. The teaching page closely follows the organization of the student reproducibles. This page also models sample text that students might generate when completing page 2 of the lesson. Finally, the teaching page includes an opportunity for students to review their classmates' work using the reproducible assessment checklist or a list customized to the lesson's writing form. Each checklist also reminds students to check for correct punctuation, spelling, and paragraph form.

Objectives & Common Core Connections

Step-by-Step Lesson With Sample Text

Student Assessment Checklist

Lesson Page 2

The second page is a student reproducible, which is the core of the lesson. Students complete this writing frame as you guide them. In many lessons, students use the completed page as the basis for a paragraph they write on a separate sheet of paper.

Introduction

Instructions

Writing Task

Although you provide a model for completing this reproducible, you'll want to encourage students to use their own ideas, words, and sentences as much as possible.

Lesson Page 3

The third page is a writing frame for independent work. It follows a format similar to the one students used for the first reproducible. Students choose their topic from the suggested list or use their own idea for the topic. In many lessons, students use the completed page as the basis for a paragraph they write on a separate sheet of paper.

Introduction

Topic Suggestions

Writing Task

Writing Lessons to Meet the Common Core: Grade 2 © 2013 by Linda Ward Beech, Scholastic Teaching Resources

Three Forms of Writing

The CCSS focus on three forms of writing—opinion, informative/explanatory, and narrative.

Opinion Writing (Standard W.2.1)

The purpose of writing opinion pieces is to convince others to think or act in a certain way, to encourage readers or listeners to share the writer's point of view, beliefs, or position. Opinion pieces are also known as persuasive writing.

I think a hamster would be a good class pet.

In developing an opinion piece, students must learn to introduce the topic, present a point of view, and supply valid reasons, facts, and expert opinions to support it. Phrases such as *I think, I believe, you should/should not* all signal persuasive writing.

We should make a class banner.

When teaching these lessons, display different examples of opinion pieces. You might include:

- editorials
- book, movie, TV, and theater reviews
- print advertisements
- letters to the editor
- feature columns

As students learn to produce different forms of writing, they are also enhancing their ability to recognize these forms in their reading.

Informative/Explanatory Writing (Standard W.2.2)

The purpose of informative/explanatory writing is to inform the reader by giving facts, explanations, and other information. Informative/explanatory writing is also called expository writing.

When writing an informative/explanatory text, students must introduce the topic and give facts, details, descriptions, and other information about the topic. The information should also be organized in a logical way. Many kinds of informative/explanatory writing require research. Sometimes illustrations are included with informative/explanatory texts.

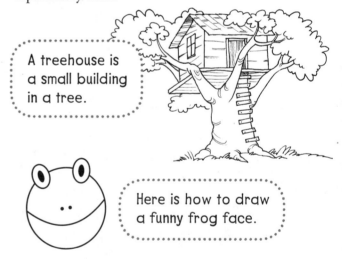

A treehouse is a small building in a tree.

Here is how to draw a funny frog face.

Display different examples of informative/explanatory writing. You might include:

- reports
- news articles
- how-to articles
- biographies
- directions
- textbooks
- magazines
- recipes

Writing Lessons to Meet the Common Core: Grade 2 © 2013 by Linda Ward Beech, Scholastic Teaching Resources

Narrative Writing (Standard W.2.3)

The purpose of narrative writing is to entertain. A narrative gives an account or a story. Usually, a narrative tells about something that happens over a period of time. Narratives can be true or imaginary.

> One day, Anya spotted a funny clown standing in the yard.

When working on a narrative, students must develop a real or imagined experience or event. They must also establish a situation or plot, create characters, and recount events in a chronological sequence. Narratives usually include descriptive details. Many include dialogue.

> Honey jumped up on the table and sneezed, "Ah-Chooo!"

> Ivan had a hat that made him invisible.

When introducing narrative writing, display different examples. You might include:

- stories
- mysteries
- fables
- fairy tales
- folktales
- science fiction
- friendly letters

Additional Writing Standards

Although this book focuses on the forms of writing called for in the CCSS, you can also incorporate the standards that relate to the production and distribution of writing and research to build and present knowledge. These standards include:

- W.2.5 Focus on a topic and strengthen writing as needed by planning, revising, and editing.

- W.2.6 Use a variety of digital tools to produce and publish writing.

- W.2.7 Participate in shared research and writing projects to produce a report.

- W.2.8 Recall information from experiences and gather information from print and digital sources.

Language Standards

In addition, you can incorporate the CCSS Language Standards that focus on the conventions of standard English grammar and usage (L.2.1) and the conventions of standard English capitalization, punctuation, and spelling (L.2.2).

Opinion Writing (Fact & Opinion)
Get a Pet

Objectives & Common Core Connections

* Differentiate between fact and opinion.
* Develop facts and opinions about a topic.

Introduction Provide each student with a copy of the fact and opinion writing frame (page 9). Read the title and first lines. Also draw attention to the illustration. Tell students that when you want others to agree with you, you have to persuade them to think the way you do. You have to convince them to share your opinion. Explain that an opinion is a point of view or what someone thinks.

Model Tell students that an opinion about a hamster might be stated like this:

* I think a hamster would be a good class pet.

Explain that opinions often begin with words such as *I think* or *I believe*. Opinions may also include words such as *should* or *would*. For example:

* I think hamsters are cute.
* A hamster would be fun to have in the room.

Point out that writers need to offer more than an opinion to get others to agree with them; they need to give reasons to support an opinion. To help students understand what kinds of reasons to include, you might say: *Often the reasons a writer gives are facts about the subject.* Explain that a fact is a statement that can be proved. Give examples of statements of fact such as:

* A hamster is small and furry.
* It keeps itself clean.
* A hamster sleeps during the day.

Guided Practice Have students complete the fact and opinion writing frame. Explain that for Part B students should write two more opinions about hamsters. They can be positive or negative. For example:

* I think we should have two hamsters.
* I don't think hamsters are much fun.

Tell students they can use the illustration on the writing frame to help them develop facts for Part B. For example:

* A hamster lives in a metal cage.
* A hamster needs food and water.

Review Check students' work to see that they completed Part A correctly—facts: 2, 3, 4; opinions: 1, 5, 6. Invite volunteers to read their sentences from Part B to the class. Have listeners use these criteria to assess other students' work:

✔ Developed opinions about a topic
✔ Included facts about a topic

Independent Practice Use the On Your Own activity (page 10) as homework or review. Encourage students to use what they learned in the lesson to complete the page. Check students' work to see that they completed Part A correctly—facts: 2, 3; opinions: 1, 4, 5, 6. For Part B, let students know that they can write negative opinions if they wish.

Writing Lessons to Meet the Common Core: Grade 2 © 2013 by Linda Ward Beech, Scholastic Teaching Resources

Get a Pet

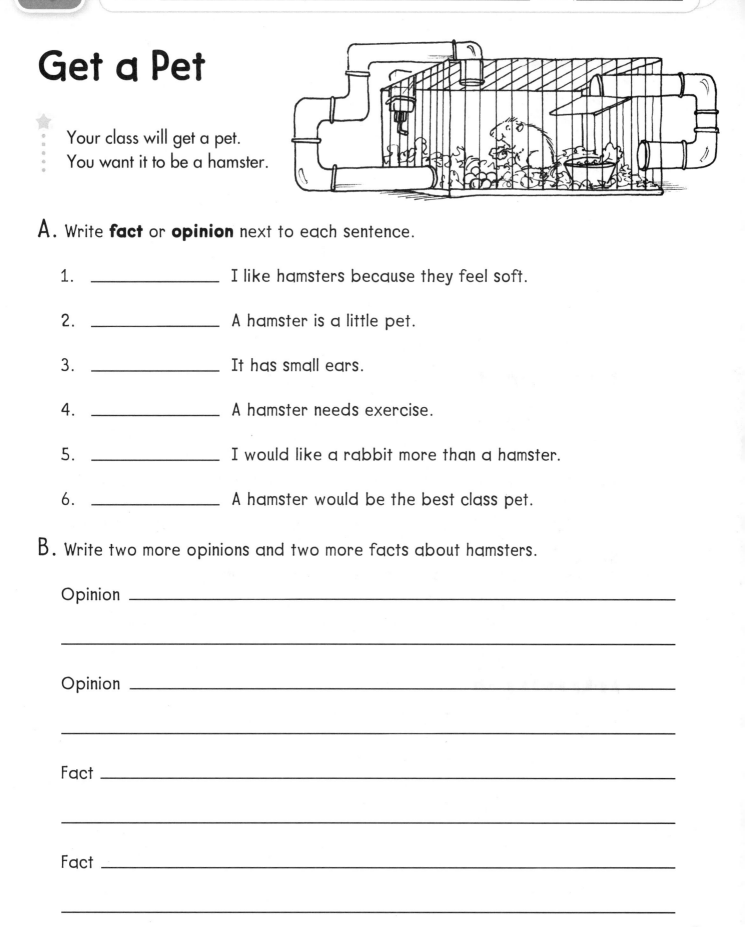

Your class will get a pet.
You want it to be a hamster.

A. Write **fact** or **opinion** next to each sentence.

1. _____ I like hamsters because they feel soft.

2. _____ A hamster is a little pet.

3. _____ It has small ears.

4. _____ A hamster needs exercise.

5. _____ I would like a rabbit more than a hamster.

6. _____ A hamster would be the best class pet.

B. Write two more opinions and two more facts about hamsters.

Opinion _____

_____

Opinion _____

_____

Fact _____

_____

Fact _____

_____

On Your Own

Jobs to Care for Our Hamster

Feed Harry Hamster.
Fill water bottle.
Clean cage.
Shred paper for cage.

What do you think about a classroom pet?

Harry's favorite foods:
seeds, apples, bananas, berries, lettuce, broccoli

A. Write **fact** or **opinion** next to each sentence.

1. _____ All classrooms should have a pet.

2. _____ Pets need care.

3. _____ A hamster eats lettuce.

4. _____ I think Harry is a good name for a hamster.

5. _____ We should read a book about taking care of pets.

6. _____ Students should take turns caring for classroom pets.

B. Write two more opinions and two more facts about hamsters.

Opinion _____

_____

Opinion _____

_____

Fact _____

_____

Fact _____

Writing Lessons to Meet the Common Core: Grade 2 © 2013 by Linda Ward Beech, Scholastic Teaching Resources

Opinion Writing
Pack a Snack

Objectives & Common Core Connections

* Introduce the topic.
* Focus on the purpose of opinion writing.
* State an opinion about the topic.
* Develop a list of reasons to support the opinion.
* Write a sentence that includes a reason for the opinion.

Introduction Provide each student with a copy of the writing frame (page 12). Read the title and first lines. Also draw attention to the pictures and word labels. Ask students to form an opinion about which snack would be best to take on a hike. Tell them that they will be writing to persuade others to agree with their opinion. Remind students that an opinion is what someone thinks or believes about something.

Model Tell students that when you write an opinion, you first introduce the topic. For example:

* What is the best snack for a hike?

Invite a volunteer to tell what snack he or she would choose. For example:

* I think raisins are the best snack.

Remind students that they want to persuade others to agree about which snack to pack for a hike. Ask: *How do you persuade someone to agree with you?* Help students understand that they should give reasons to support an opinion. For example:

* easy to carry
* healthy
* sweet and tasty

Encourage students to contribute other reasons for taking raisins on a hike. Talk about which are the most convincing reasons.

Guide students in developing a sentence using one of the reasons. For example:

* A box of raisins would be easy to carry on a hike.

Guided Practice Have students complete the writing frame. Instruct them to introduce the topic, focus on the writing purpose, state an opinion, and list at least three reasons to support their opinion. Point out that students can express a different opinion if they wish, choosing either carrots or cheese. They should give appropriate reasons to support these choices.

Review Invite volunteers to read their finished pages to the class. Have listeners use items 1–5 on the assessment checklist (page 62) to evaluate the effectiveness of other students' work.

Independent Practice Use the On Your Own activity (page 13) as homework or review. Encourage students to use what they learned in the lesson to complete the page. Explain that students can choose a food from the Idea Box or think of their own snack idea.

Pack a Snack

★ You need a good snack for a hike.
Which one will you pack?

- Introduce the topic.
- Think about your writing purpose.
- State your opinion.
- List reasons to support your opinion.
- Write a practice sentence.

Raisins

Cheese

Carrots

Topic _____

Writing Purpose _____

_____

Opinion _____

_____

Reasons _____

_____

_____

Practice Sentence _____

_____

_____

Writing Lessons to Meet the Common Core: Grade 2 © 2013 by Linda Ward Beech, Scholastic Teaching Resources

Name _____ Date _____

On Your Own

Which would be the best snack for after school?
Choose a food from the Idea Box or think of another food.
Complete this page to get others to agree with you.

Idea Box

○ Pretzels   ○ Grapes   ○ Yogurt   ○ My Idea:

_____

_____

Topic _____

Writing Purpose _____

_____

Opinion _____

_____

Reasons _____

_____

_____

_____

Sentence _____

_____

_____

Opinion Writing
Community Visit

Objectives & Common Core Connections

* Introduce the topic.
* Focus on the purpose of opinion writing.
* State an opinion about the topic.
* Develop a list of reasons to support the opinion.
* Write sentences that include reasons for the opinion.

Introduction Provide each student with a copy of the writing frame (page 15). Read the title and first lines. Also draw attention to the illustrations. Ask students to think about which place—the firehouse or police station—they would most like to visit. Explain that they will be writing sentences to persuade others to share their opinion. Reinforce that an opinion is someone's point of view or belief about something.

Model Tell students that they should begin by introducing the topic. Write the topic in sentence form on the board. For example:

* What place in the community should we visit?

Focus students on the purpose of writing: to persuade others to agree with their opinion. Invite a volunteer to give you an opinion. For example:

* I think we should go to the firehouse.

Point out that once a writer offers an opinion, he or she should give reasons to support it. Ask students to think of reasons to go to the firehouse. For example:

* see fire trucks
* try on boots and hats
* learn about fighting fires

Encourage students to come up with other reasons, then coach them in using the reasons to develop complete sentences. For example:

* We could see the different kinds of fire trucks.
* It would be fun to try on a firefighter's hat.
* We could learn about fighting fires.

Guided Practice Have students complete the writing frame. Point out that they can choose either the firehouse or the police station as their topic. Encourage students to use their own words and sentence structure.

Review Invite volunteers to read their finished pages to the class. Have listeners use items 1–5 on the assessment checklist (page 62) to evaluate the effectiveness of other students' work.

Independent Practice Use the On Your Own activity (page 16) as homework or review. Encourage students to use what they learned in the lesson to complete the page. Explain that they can choose a community place from the Idea Box or use their own idea.

Name _____ Date _____

Community Visit

⭐ Your class will visit a place in the community. Should it be the firehouse or the police station?

- Introduce the topic.
- Think about your writing purpose.
- State your opinion.
- List reasons to support your opinion.
- Write practice sentences with reasons.

Topic _____

Writing Purpose _____

_____

Opinion _____

_____

Reasons _____

_____

_____

Practice Sentences _____

_____

_____

_____

_____

Name _____ Date _____

On Your Own

What place in the community would you like to visit?
Choose a place from the Idea Box or think of another place.
Complete this page to get others to agree with you.

Idea Box

○ Library   ○ Park   ○ Museum   ○ My Idea: _____

LIBRARY   PARK   MUSEUM   _____

Topic _____

Writing Purpose _____

_____

Opinion _____

_____

Reasons _____

_____

_____

Sentences _____

_____

_____

_____

Writing Lessons to Meet the Common Core: Grade 2 © 2013 by Linda Ward Beech, Scholastic Teaching Resources

Opinion Writing
For Our Class

Objectives & Common Core Connections

* Introduce the topic.
* Focus on the purpose of opinion writing.
* State an opinion about the topic.
* Present a list of reasons to support the opinion.
* Write sentences that include reasons for the opinion.
* Write a paragraph that expresses an opinion.

Introduction Provide each student with a copy of the writing frame (page 18). Read the title and first lines. Also draw attention to the speech balloons. Ask students to think about what they would like to create—a song or banner—to honor the class. Explain that they will be writing a paragraph to persuade others to share their opinion. Reinforce that an opinion is someone's point of view or idea about something.

Model Review that a paragraph is a group of sentences about the same topic. Then, tell students that they should introduce the topic. Write a sample topic sentence on the board. For example:

* We're going to honor our class.

Ask a volunteer to offer an opinion about writing a song or making a banner. For example:

* We should make a class banner.

Point out that once a writer offers an opinion, he or she must give reasons to support it. Ask students to think of reasons to make a class banner. For example:

* can display it for everyone to see
* will call attention to our class
* reminder that we're a great class

Encourage the class to come up with other reasons, then coach students in using the reasons to develop complete sentences. For example:

* We can display the banner for everyone to see.
* It will tell people about our class.
* The banner will be a reminder that we're a great class.

Guided Practice Have students complete the writing frame. Point out that they can choose either the banner or the song as their topic. Encourage students to use their own words and sentences.

Review Invite volunteers to read their finished paragraphs to the class. Have listeners use items 1–5 and 7 on the assessment checklist (page 62) to evaluate the effectiveness of other students' work.

Independent Practice Use the On Your Own activity (page 19) as homework or practice. Encourage students to use what they learned in the lesson to complete it. Explain that they can choose a way to show school spirit from the Idea Box or use their own idea.

Name _____ Date _____

For Our Class

Let's make
a class
banner.

Let's have
a class
song.

⭐ You want to honor your class.
Will you design a banner or write a song?

- Introduce the topic.
- Think about your writing purpose.
- State your opinion.
- List reasons to support your opinion.
- Write practice sentences with reasons.
- Write your paragraph on another sheet of paper.

Topic _____

Writing Purpose _____

_____

Opinion _____

_____

Reasons _____

_____

_____

Practice Sentences _____

_____

_____

_____

Writing Lessons to Meet the Common Core: Grade 2 © 2013 by Linda Ward Beech, Scholastic Teaching Resources

Name _____ Date _____

On Your Own

What would you do to show school spirit?
Choose an idea from the Idea Box or think of one of your own.
Complete this page.
Then, write your paragraph on another sheet of paper.
Get others to agree with you.

Idea Box

○ Think Up a School Motto   ○ My Idea: _____

○ Make Up a School Handshake   _____

○ Write a School Cheer   _____

Topic _____

Writing Purpose _____

_____

Opinion _____

_____

Reasons _____

_____

_____

Sentences _____

_____

_____

_____

Opinion Writing
Super Socks

Objectives & Common Core Connections

* Introduce the topic.
* Focus on the purpose of opinion writing.
* State an opinion about the topic.
* Present reasons to support the opinion.
* Write sentences using linking words to connect the reasons and opinion.
* Write a paragraph that expresses an opinion.

Introduction Provide each student with a copy of the writing frame (page 21). Read the title and first lines. Then, have students study the picture and read the speech balloons. Encourage them to think of other things they might say about socks they designed. Explain that they will write a paragraph to persuade others to share their opinion. Review that an opinion is someone's point of view or idea about something.

Model Review that a paragraph is a group of sentences about the same topic. Explain that in an opinion piece, writers should introduce the topic. Write the topic in sentence form on the board. For example:

* I designed some socks.

Invite a volunteer to suggest what the designer's opinion about the socks might be. For example:

* I think they are great socks.

Remind students that they are writing to persuade their readers to agree with them about the socks. Ask: *How do you persuade someone to agree with you?* Help students recall that they should offer reasons. For example:

* fun to wear
* unusual
* people will notice
* have happy toes

Encourage students to come up with other reasons, then talk about the different reasons and how they might be useful in persuading someone to think the socks are great. Coach students in developing complete sentences from the reasons. Model how some reasons and the opinion might be connected with linking words, such as *because* or *also* (underlined below). For example:

* These socks will be cool to wear.
* People will notice them <u>because</u> they're unusual.
* I <u>also</u> like the happy toes on these socks.

Guided Practice Have students complete the writing frame. Encourage them to use their own wording and sentence structure and to underline the linking words they add to connect their reasons and opinion.

Review Invite volunteers to read their finished paragraphs to the class. Have listeners use items 1–6 and 8 on the assessment checklist (page 62) to evaluate the effectiveness of other students' work.

Independent Practice Use the On Your Own activity (page 22) as homework or review. Encourage students to use what they learned in the lesson to complete it. Explain that they can choose a topic from the Idea Box or use their own idea. Provide paper so students can draw a picture of their design before they write about it. Also remind them to underline the linking words they use.

Name _____ Date _____

Super Socks

⭐ You design some new socks.
You think they're great.
How can you get others to agree with you?

- Introduce the topic.
- Think about your writing purpose.
- State your opinion.
- Give reasons to support it.
- Write practice sentences. Use linking words.
- Write your paragraph on another sheet of paper.

We're different.

We're cool!

Topic _____

Writing Purpose _____

_____

Opinion _____

_____

Reasons _____

_____

_____

Practice Sentences _____

_____

_____

_____

Name _____ Date _____

On Your Own

Pretend you are a great designer. Choose something to design from the Idea Box or think of another kind of clothing.
Draw a picture of your design. Then, complete this page.
Use linking words. Write your paragraph on another sheet of paper.
Get others to agree that your design is great.

Idea Box

○ Sneakers   ○ Mittens   ○ Cap   ○ My Idea:

_____

_____

Topic _____

Writing Purpose _____

_____

Opinion _____

_____

Reasons _____

_____

_____

Sentences _____

_____

_____

_____

Opinion Writing
Be a Bear

Objectives & Common Core Connections

* Introduce the topic.
* Focus on the purpose of opinion writing.
* State an opinion about the topic.
* Present reasons to support the opinion.
* Write sentences that include reasons for the opinion.
* Provide a concluding statement
* Write a paragraph that expresses an opinion.

Introduction Provide each student with a copy of the writing frame (page 24). Read the title and first lines. Then, draw attention to the picture and speech balloons. Explain that students will pretend to be the bear. They will write a paragraph to persuade the zookeeper to agree with them. Remind students that an opinion is a point of view or idea about something.

Model Review that a paragraph is a group of sentences about the same topic. Model an introduction and opinion for the beginning of the paragraph. For example:

* I ran away from the zoo.
* I don't want to go back!

Remind students that they, as the bear, are writing to persuade the zookeeper to agree with their opinion. Ask them to come up with reasons to support this opinion. For example:

* get bored in the zoo
* like to play with other bears in the woods
* don't like living in cage
* want to be free

Talk about the different ideas and how they might be useful in persuading the zookeeper to let the bear go. Coach students in developing complete sentences from the reasons. For example:

* It's boring to live in the zoo.
* I want to play with the bears who live in the woods.
* I don't like living in a cage.
* I want to be a free bear!

Tell students that a good opinion usually has a concluding sentence. This sentence restates the writer's opinion. For example:

* So now you know why I don't want to live in the zoo.

Guided Practice Have students complete the writing frame. Encourage them to use their own wording and sentence structure.

Review Invite volunteers to read their finished paragraphs to the class. Have listeners use items 1–5, 7, and 8 on the assessment checklist (page 62) to evaluate the effectiveness of other students' work.

Independent Practice Use the On Your Own activity (page 25) as homework or review. Encourage students to use what they learned in the lesson to complete it. Explain that they can choose an animal with an opinion from the Idea Box or think of one of their own. Provide additional paper and suggest that students draw a picture to go with their paragraph.

Name _____ Date _____

Be a Bear

Pretend you are a bear who has
run away from a zoo.
You don't want to go back.
How can you get the zookeeper
to agree with you?

> You live in
> the zoo.

> No, no!

- Introduce the topic.
- Think about your writing purpose.
- State your opinion.
- Write sentences with reasons to support your opinion.
- Write a concluding sentence.
- Write your paragraph on another sheet of paper.

Topic _____

Writing Purpose _____

_____

Opinion _____

_____

Sentences With Reasons _____

_____

_____

_____

Concluding Sentence _____

_____

Writing Lessons to Meet the Common Core: Grade 2 © 2013 by Linda Ward Beech, Scholastic Teaching Resources

Name _____ Date _____

On Your Own

Pretend you are an animal with a strong opinion. Choose one of the animals in the Idea Box or think of another animal. Then, complete this page. Write your paragraph on another sheet of paper. Get others to agree with you.

Idea Box

- ○ Elephant who ran away from the circus
- ○ Horse who doesn't want to be in a horse show
- ○ Turkey who doesn't want to be Thanksgiving dinner

- ○ My Idea: _____

_____

Topic _____

Writing Purpose _____

_____

Opinion _____

_____

Sentences With Reasons _____

_____

_____

_____

Concluding Sentence _____

_____

Informative Writing (Main Idea)
Get the Idea

Objectives & Common Core Connections

❊ Identify main ideas.

❊ Develop main idea sentences about topics.

Introduction Provide each student with a copy of the writing frame (page 27). Read the title. Then, draw attention to the idea web at the top of the page. Explain that the information in the web can be used in a paragraph to inform readers about what a parka is.

Model You might say: *The parka would be the main idea of the paragraph. The main idea is the most important idea in the paragraph.* Give as an example:

• A parka is a warm jacket.

Point out that a writer must develop a main idea by giving more information. You might say: *The information in the smaller circles tells more about the main idea. The words tell more about what a parka is like.*

Guided Practice Have students complete the writing frame. Explain that they should write a main idea in each of the webs and then write a main idea sentence for each web. For example:

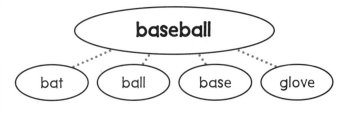

You use certain things to play baseball.

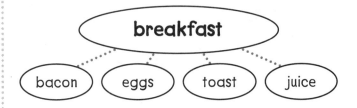

Some foods are popular at breakfast.

Review Invite volunteers to read their main ideas and sentences to the class. Have listeners use these criteria to assess other students' work:

✔ Identified main ideas
✔ Developed main idea sentences

Independent Practice Use the On Your Own activity (page 28) as homework or review. Encourage students to use what they learned in the lesson to complete the page. For #2, explain that they can choose a topic from the Idea Box or use their own idea.

Name _____ Date _____

Get the Idea

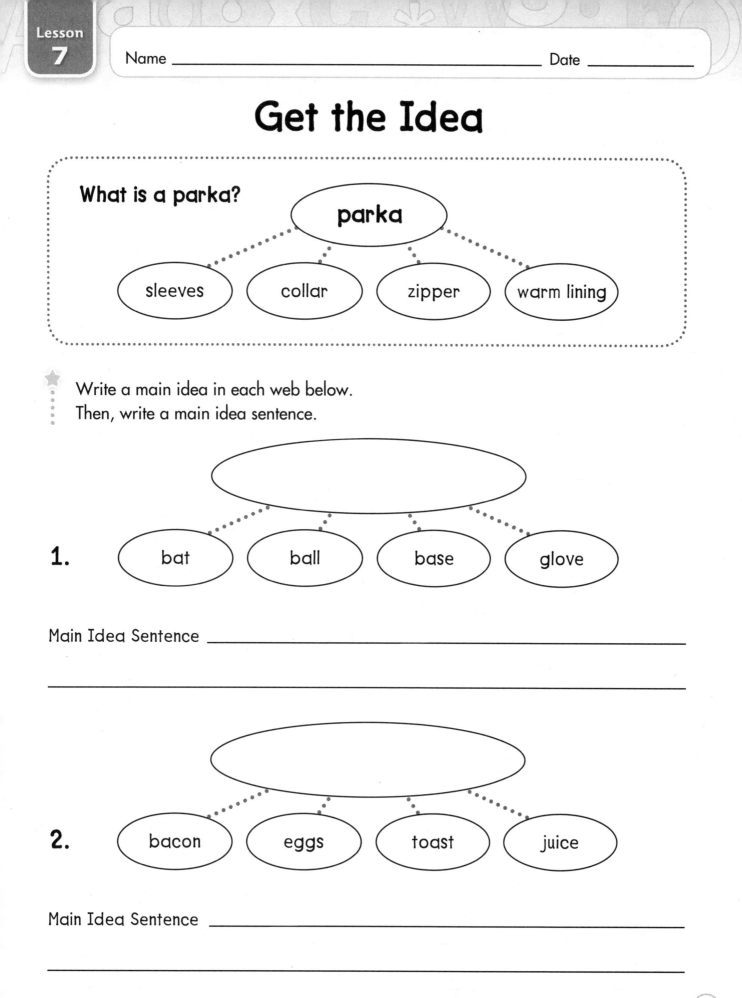

What is a parka?

parka
sleeves   collar   zipper   warm lining

Write a main idea in each web below.
Then, write a main idea sentence.

1.
bat   ball   base   glove

Main Idea Sentence _____

_____

2.
bacon   eggs   toast   juice

Main Idea Sentence _____

_____

Name _____ Date _____

⭐ On Your
⭐ Own ⭐

1. Write a main idea in the web below.
Then, write a main idea sentence.

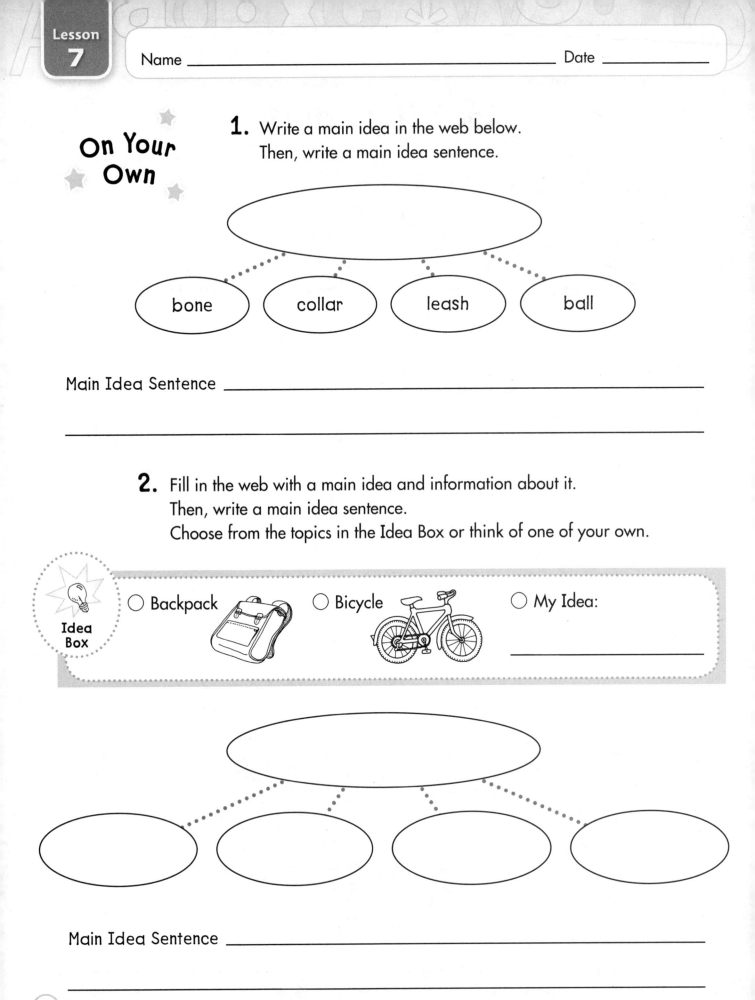

bone   collar   leash   ball

Main Idea Sentence _____

_____

2. Fill in the web with a main idea and information about it.
Then, write a main idea sentence.
Choose from the topics in the Idea Box or think of one of your own.

Idea
Box

○ Backpack   ○ Bicycle   ○ My Idea:
_____

Main Idea Sentence _____

_____

Informative Writing
In the Treetops

* Introduce a topic with a main idea sentence.
* Focus on the purpose of informative writing.
* Use facts to develop the topic.
* Write sentences using the facts.

Introduction Provide each student with a copy of the writing frame (page 30). Read the title and first line. Also draw attention to the illustration. Tell students that they will write sentences to tell what a treehouse is. Explain that the purpose of informative writing is to tell the reader about the topic.

Model You might say: *The picture shows a treehouse. You can see that it's a little building in a tree. That will be the topic you will write about. You can introduce the topic by writing a main idea sentence such as:*

* A treehouse is a small building in a tree.

Explain that the next step is to tell more about the topic. Remind students that their purpose is to inform readers about the topic. Suggest that they use the illustration for more information. For example:

* made of strong wood
* has a platform or floor
* has walls
* has a ladder

Encourage students to contribute other facts and information about treehouses. Then, coach them in using the facts and information to develop complete sentences. For example:

* A treehouse is made of strong wood.
* It has a floor and walls.
* A treehouse has a ladder so you can get up to it.

Guided Practice Have students complete the writing frame. Encourage them to use their own words and sentence structure when they write their practice sentences.

Review Invite volunteers to share their pages with the class. Have listeners use items 1–4 on the assessment checklist (page 63) to evaluate the effectiveness of other students' work.

Independent Practice Use the On Your Own activity (page 31) as homework or review. Encourage students to use what they learned in the lesson to complete the page. Explain that they can choose a house from the Idea Box or use their own idea.

In the Treetops

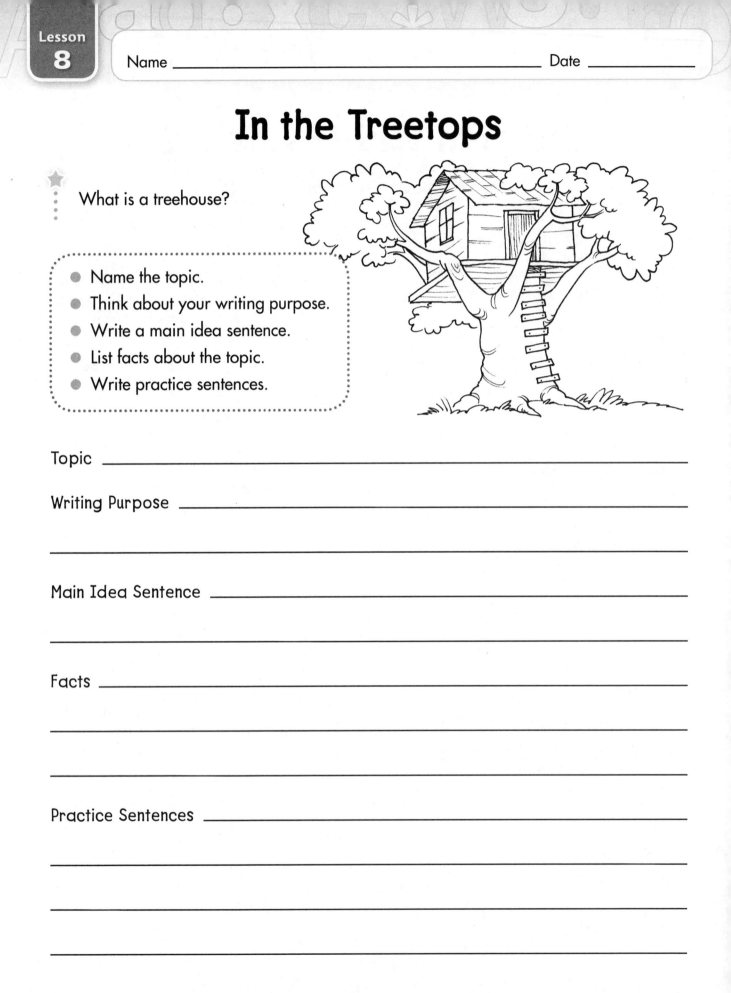

⭐ What is a treehouse?

- Name the topic.
- Think about your writing purpose.
- Write a main idea sentence.
- List facts about the topic.
- Write practice sentences.

Topic _____

Writing Purpose _____

_____

Main Idea Sentence _____

_____

Facts _____

_____

_____

Practice Sentences _____

_____

_____

_____

Name _____ Date _____

On Your Own

Choose a kind of house from the Idea Box
or think of one of your own.
Complete the page to tell what this house is like.

Idea Box

○ Doghouse   ○ Dollhouse   ○ Birdhouse   ○ My Idea:
_____
_____

Topic _____

Writing Purpose _____

_____

Main Idea Sentence _____

_____

Facts _____

_____

_____

Sentences _____

_____

_____

_____

_____

Informative Writing
Go Fly a Kite

Objectives & Common Core Connections

* Introduce a topic with a main idea sentence.
* Focus on the purpose of informative writing.
* Use facts to develop the topic.
* Write sentences using the facts.
* Write an informative paragraph.

Introduction Provide each student with a copy of the writing frame (page 33). Read the title and first line. Also draw attention to the illustration. Tell students that they will write a paragraph telling what a kite is. Remind them that the purpose of informative writing is to give information to the reader. Review that a paragraph is a group of sentences about the same topic.

Model You might say: *The picture shows a girl with a kite. That will be the topic you write about. You can introduce the topic with a main idea sentence such as:*

* A kite is something you can fly in the air.

Explain that the next step is to tell more about the topic. Remind students that their purpose is to inform. Suggest that they use the illustration for more information about the topic. You might say: *You can see that the kite has a frame and material covering it. This must be light material because the kite is in the air. You can also see that the girl is holding onto a line to fly the kite and that she is running to fly the kite.* List the information you have developed:

* has a frame covered with light material
* has a string called a line
* you run to catch wind and fly kite

Encourage students to contribute other facts and information about kites. Then, coach them in using the facts and information to develop complete sentences. For example:

* A kite has a frame covered by light material.
* It has a line that you hold.
* When you run, the wind makes the kite fly.

Guided Practice Once you have used the sentences to develop a sample paragraph, have students complete the writing frame. Encourage them to use their own words and sentences.

Review Invite volunteers to read their finished paragraphs to the class. Have listeners use items 1–4 and 8 on the assessment checklist (page 63) to evaluate the effectiveness of other students' work.

Independent Practice Use the On Your Own activity (page 34) as homework or review. Encourage students to use what they learned in the lesson to complete it. Tell them they can choose a toy from the Idea Box or use their own idea. It may be helpful for students to find or draw a picture of their toy before writing about it.

Writing Lessons to Meet the Common Core: Grade 2 © 2013 by Linda Ward Beech, Scholastic Teaching Resources

Name _____ Date _____

Go Fly a Kite

What is a kite?

- Name the topic.
- Think about your writing purpose.
- Write a main idea sentence.
- List facts about the topic.
- Write practice sentences.
- Write your paragraph on another sheet of paper.

Topic _____

Writing Purpose _____

_____

Main Idea Sentence _____

_____

Facts _____

_____

_____

Practice Sentences _____

_____

_____

_____

Name _____ Date _____

On Your Own

Choose a toy from the Idea Box or think of one of your own.
Complete the page to tell what this toy is like.
Then, write your paragraph on another sheet of paper.

Idea
Box

○ Puppet   ○ Yo-yo   ○ Jump Rope   ○ My Idea:

_____

_____

Topic _____

Writing Purpose _____

_____

Main Idea Sentence _____

_____

Facts _____

_____

_____

Sentences _____

_____

_____

_____

Explanatory Writing
Fruit Flower

Objectives & Common Core Connections

* Introduce a topic with a main idea sentence.
* Focus on the purpose of explanatory writing.
* List materials and steps.
* Include an illustration.
* Write an explanatory paragraph.

Introduction Provide each student with a copy of the writing frame (page 36). Have students read the title and first line. Also draw attention to the shapes of the fruits and the design made from them. Point out that an explanatory paragraph can tell how to do something. Inform students that they will write a paragraph telling how to make a fruit dessert that looks like a flower. Review that a paragraph is a group of sentences about the same topic.

Model Help students begin their explanation by writing a main idea sentence. For example:

You can use pieces of fruit to make a flower design.

Tell students that when explaining how to do something, they will need to list materials and steps. For example:

* collect orange slice, green grapes, plate
* put orange slice on plate
* place grapes around orange slice

Point out that the steps must be given in a logical order so someone can follow them.

Coach students in developing complete and more informative sentences to use in a paragraph. For example:

* You need an orange slice, some grapes, and a plate.
* Put the orange slice in the center of the plate.
* Place the grapes around the orange to make a flower.

Mention that it is a good idea to include an illustration with some explanations. Talk with students about how the illustration on page 36 helps a reader know what to do.

Guided Practice Once you have developed a sample paragraph, have students complete the writing frame. Encourage them to use their own words and sentence structure. Provide additional paper for students' paragraphs and drawings.

Review Invite volunteers to read their finished paragraphs to the class. Have listeners use items 1, 2, 5, 7, and 8 on the assessment checklist (page 63) to evaluate the effectiveness of other students' work.

Independent Practice Use the On Your Own activity (page 37) as homework or review. Encourage students to use what they learned in the lesson to complete it. Tell them they can choose the fruit design from the Idea Box or use their own idea. Remind them that they will need to decide what fruits to use. Have students draw a picture of their arrangement before writing about it. (Note: The Fruit Caterpillar uses banana slices for the body and blueberries for eyes.)

Fruit Flower

⭐ How can you use fruit to make a flower design?

- Name the topic.
- Think about your writing purpose.
- Write a main idea sentence.
- Name the materials and steps.
- Write practice sentences.
- Draw a picture and write your paragraph on another sheet of paper.

Topic _____

Writing Purpose _____

Main Idea Sentence _____

_____

Materials _____   Steps _____

_____   _____

_____   _____

_____   _____

Practice Sentences _____

_____

_____

_____

_____

Name _____ Date _____

On Your Own

Complete the page to tell how to make a Fruit Caterpillar. Or think of your own fruit design. Draw a picture of your fruit design and write your paragraph on another sheet of paper.

Idea Box

○ Fruit Caterpillar   ○ My Idea:

_____

_____

_____

Topic _____

Writing Purpose _____

Main Idea Sentence _____

_____

Materials _____   Steps _____

_____   _____

_____   _____

_____   _____

Sentences _____

_____

_____

_____

Explanatory Writing
Funny Faces

Objectives & Common Core Connections

* Introduce a topic with a main idea sentence.
* Focus on the purpose of explanatory writing.
* List materials and steps.
* Include an illustration.
* Write an explanatory paragraph.

Introduction Provide each student with a copy of the writing frame (page 39). Read the title and first line. Also have students study the illustration. Point out that an explanatory paragraph can tell how to do something. Tell students that they will write a paragraph telling how to draw a funny frog face. Review that a paragraph is a group of sentences about the same topic.

Model Help students begin their explanation by writing a main idea sentence. For example:

Here is how to draw a funny frog face.

Tell students that when explaining how to do something, they will need to list materials and steps. For example:

* collect jar lid, paper, pencil
* trace a circle around lid
* draw eyes, nose, and mouth

Point out that the steps must be given in a logical order so someone can follow them. Coach students in developing complete and more informative sentences to use in a paragraph. For example:

* Collect a jar lid, paper, and a pencil.
* Place the jar lid on the paper.
* Trace a circle around the lid.
* Draw eyes, a nose, and a mouth on the circle.

Mention that it is a good idea to include an illustration with some explanations. Talk with students about how the illustration on page 39 helps a reader know what to do.

Guided Practice Once you have developed a sample paragraph, have students complete the writing frame. Encourage them to use their own words and sentence structure. Provide additional paper for students' paragraphs and frog drawings.

Review Invite volunteers to read their finished paragraphs to the class. Have listeners use items 1, 2, 5, 7, and 8 on the assessment checklist (page 63) to evaluate the effectiveness of other students' work.

Independent Practice Use the On Your Own activity (page 40) as homework or review. Encourage students to use what they learned in the lesson to complete it. Tell them they can choose an animal from the Idea Box or use their own idea. Have students draw a picture of their animal before writing about it. Provide paper for students' illustrations.

Writing Lessons to Meet the Common Core: Grade 2 © 2013 by Linda Ward Beech, Scholastic Teaching Resources

Funny Faces

How can you draw a frog face?

- Name the topic.
- Think about your writing purpose.
- Write a main idea sentence.
- Name the materials and steps.
- Write practice sentences.
- Draw a picture and write your paragraph on another sheet of paper.

Topic _____

Writing Purpose _____

Main Idea Sentence _____

_____

Materials _____   Steps _____

_____   _____

_____   _____

_____   _____

Practice Sentences _____

_____

_____

_____

Name _____ Date _____

On Your Own

Choose an animal from the Idea Box or think of one of your own. Complete the page to tell how to draw the animal. Draw a picture of your animal and write your paragraph on another sheet of paper.

Idea Box

○ Monkey   ○ Bear   ○ Owl   ○ My Idea:

_____

_____

Topic _____

Writing Purpose _____

Main Idea Sentence _____

_____

Materials _____   Steps _____

_____   _____

_____   _____

_____   _____

Sentences _____

_____

_____

_____

_____

Writing Lessons to Meet the Common Core: Grade 2 © 2013 by Linda Ward Beech, Scholastic Teaching Resources

Informative Writing
Fire-Drill Facts

Objectives & Common Core Connections

❄ Introduce a topic with a main idea sentence.

❄ Focus on the purpose of informative writing.

❄ Use facts to develop the topic.

❄ Write sentences using the facts.

❄ Include a concluding sentence.

❄ Write an informative paragraph.

Introduction Provide each student with a copy of the writing frame (page 42). Read the title and first line. Also draw attention to the illustration. Tell students that they will write a paragraph telling about fire-drill rules. Remind them that the purpose of informative writing is to give information to the reader. Review that a paragraph is a group of sentences about the same topic.

Model You might say: *The topic is what to do during a school fire drill. You can introduce the topic with a main idea sentence such as:*

A fire drill helps everyone know what to do if there's a fire.

Remind students that the next step is to tell more about the topic. Suggest that they use the illustration and their own knowledge to develop facts and information about fire-drill procedures. For example:

• leave room in an orderly line

• follow fire-drill route to assembly place

• no talking

• wait for all-clear signal

Coach students in using the facts and information to develop complete sentences. For example:

• Leave the classroom in an orderly line.

• Follow the fire-drill route to your assembly place.

• Do not talk!

• Wait for the all-clear signal before returning to your classroom.

Tell students that an informative paragraph usually has a concluding sentence. This sentence retells or summarizes information in the paragraph. For example:

• A fire drill is a good way to practice safety.

Guided Practice Once you have developed a sample paragraph, have students complete the writing frame. Encourage them to use their own words and sentences as well as other facts and information they know about fire drills.

Review Invite volunteers to read their finished paragraphs to the class. Have listeners use items 1–4, 6, and 8 on the assessment checklist (page 63) to evaluate the effectiveness of other students' work.

Independent Practice Use the On Your Own activity (page 43) as homework or review. Encourage students to use what they learned in the lesson to complete it. Tell them they can choose a safety topic from the Idea Box or use their own idea.

Name _____ Date _____

Fire-Drill Facts

What should you do in a fire drill?

- Name the topic.
- Think about your writing purpose.
- Write a main idea sentence.
- List facts about the topic.
- Write practice sentences and a concluding sentence.
- Write your paragraph on another sheet of paper.

Topic _____

Writing Purpose _____

_____

Main Idea Sentence _____

_____

Facts _____

_____

_____

Practice Sentences _____

_____

_____

_____

Concluding Sentence _____

_____

Writing Lessons to Meet the Common Core: Grade 2 © 2013 by Linda Ward Beech, Scholastic Teaching Resources

Name _____ Date _____

On Your Own

Choose a safety topic from the Idea Box or think of one of your own. Complete the page to tell what rules to follow. Then, write your paragraph on another sheet of paper.

Idea Box

○ Crossing a Street   ○ Riding a Bike   ○ On a Playground   ○ My Idea:

_____

_____

Topic _____

Writing Purpose _____

_____

Main Idea Sentence _____

_____

Facts _____

_____

_____

Sentences _____

_____

_____

_____

Concluding Sentence _____

Narrative Writing (Sequence)
In Order

Introduction Provide each student with a copy of the writing frame (page 45). Read the title and first line. Also draw attention to the illustrations. Point out that the pictures show a series of events in the order, or sequence, in which they happened. Tell students that when you write a story or narrative, you use sequence to help the reader understand what is happening. If you tell things out of order, they don't make sense.

Model You might say: *You can make up a narrative based on what you see in the pictures. A narrative is a story or account of something. You usually write a narrative to entertain the reader.* Have students follow the pictures as you give sample sentences about the story in the pictures. Point out that you are going to give the girls in the pictures names.

- Rose and Anna saw the ice cream truck.
- Rose got an ice cream cone, and Anna got a popsicle.
- Rose dropped her ice cream.
- Anna broke her popsicle in half and shared it with Rose.

Guided Practice Have students complete the writing frame. For Part A, students should read the sentences carefully and then number

them 1–4 to identify the sequence. (Answers— top to bottom: 2, 4, 3, 1) For Part B, they should number the pictures 1–4 to show the best sequence, and then use that sequence to write a sentence for each event. (They can use another sheet of paper to write their sentences, if needed.) Encourage students to use their own words and ideas. (Answers—2, 4, 1, 3)

- Maria went to the library.
- She chose a book that looked good.
- She checked it out at the desk.
- Maria sat in a big chair and read her book.

Review Invite volunteers to read their sentences from Part B to the class. Have listeners use these criteria to assess other students work:

✔ Identified sequence of events for a narrative
✔ Wrote sentences in order

Independent Practice Use the On Your Own activity (page 46) as homework or review. Encourage students to use what they learned in the lesson to complete the page. (Answers—Part A: **1.** 2, 4, 3, 1; **2.** 2, 3, 4, 1; Part B: 3, 2, 4, 1)

Name _____ Date _____

In Order

The pictures tell a story in order.

A. Number the sentences 1 to 4 to show the best order.

_____ Mr. Silva went to the store. _____ Mr. Silva filled his cart.

_____ Mr. Silva paid at the counter. _____ Mr. Silva made a list.

B. Number the pictures 1 to 4 to show the best order.
Then, write a sentence for each picture, starting with number 1.

_____

_____

_____

_____

_____

On Your Own

A. Number each set of sentences 1 to 4 to show the best order.

1 _____ Troy got a sponge.

_____ Troy poured some more milk.

_____ Troy cleaned up the milk.

_____ Troy spilled his milk.

2 _____ Dad bought some popcorn.

_____ Dad and Jen found seats.

_____ Dad and Jen watched the movie.

_____ Dad paid for the tickets.

B. Number the pictures 1 to 4 to show the best order.
Then, write a sentence for each picture, starting with number 1.

_____

_____

_____

_____

_____

Writing Lessons to Meet the Common Core: Grade 2 © 2013 by Linda Ward Beech, Scholastic Teaching Resources

Narrative Writing
Fresh Eggs

Objectives & Common Core Connections

* Focus on the purpose of narrative writing.
* Develop a good opening sentence.
* Write sentences in sequence to recount a series of events.

Introduction Provide each student with a copy of the writing frame (page 48). Read the title and first line. Also draw attention to the illustrations. Point out that the pictures show a series of events. Remind students that when you write a narrative, you use sequence to help the reader understand what is happening. Review that a narrative is a story or an account of something that is written to entertain the reader.

Model You might say: *You can make up sentences for a narrative based on these pictures.* Explain that you're going to begin by developing a good opening sentence. Tell students that you are going to give the boy in the pictures a name. For example:

* Nanda's family had some hens.

Point out that the pictures show a boy going to a place where he gets food, collecting the food, having his mother cook the food, and eating the food. Have students follow the pictures as you suggest sample sentences for each picture. For example:

* Each morning Nanda went to the henhouse.
* He collected eggs.
* Nanda's mother cooked the eggs.
* Nanda had fresh eggs for breakfast.

Guided Practice Have students complete the writing frame. Encourage them to use their own words and sentences.

Review Invite volunteers to read their finished paragraphs to the class. Have listeners use items 1, 2, and 4 on the assessment checklist (page 64) to evaluate the effectiveness of other students' sentences.

Independent Practice Use the On Your Own activity (page 49) as homework or review. Encourage students to use what they learned in the lesson to complete the page. Tell them they can choose a food gathering topic from the Idea Box or use their own idea. Point out that students can follow a sequence similar to the one they used on the Fresh Eggs page—going to get food, getting food, preparing it, and eating it. Students may want to draw a sequence of four pictures first and then write a sentence for each picture. (Provide additional paper for students to draw their pictures.)

Fresh Eggs

Use the pictures to tell a story.

| 1 | 2 | 3 | 4 |

- Focus on your writing purpose.
- Write a good opening sentence.
- Write four sentences in order to tell what is happening.

Writing Purpose _____

_____

Opening Sentence _____

_____

Sentences in Order _____

_____

_____

_____

_____

_____

Name _____ Date _____

On Your Own

Choose a story topic about getting food from the Idea Box.
Or think of one of your own.
Complete the page.
Draw pictures to go with your sentences.

Idea Box

○ Girl Goes Fishing

○ Boy and Mother Pick Oranges From Tree

○ Man Picks Melon Off Vine on Ground

○ My Idea: _____

_____

_____

Writing Purpose _____

_____

Opening Sentence _____

_____

Sentences in Order _____

_____

_____

_____

_____

_____

_____

Narrative Writing
Clown Surprise

Introduction Provide each student with a copy of the writing frame (page 51). Read the title and first line. Also draw attention to the illustration and speech balloon. Tell students that they will write a narrative about the picture. Remind them that a narrative is a story or account of something that is written to entertain the reader.

Model You might say: *You can make up a story based on the picture.* Explain that you're going to begin by thinking of a good opening sentence. Point out that you are going to give the girl in the picture a name. For example:

- Anya liked to look out the window.

Have students help you develop a story based on the picture. Remind them that the events should be told in order. Ask questions, such as: *What does Anya see? What are the tickets for? Who is the clown?* For example:

- sees a clown
- clown gives Anya two tickets
- tickets are for the circus
- clown is Anya's aunt

Coach students in developing complete sentences for the story that elaborate on the events and give the reader more information. Guide them in adding descriptive words and details (underlined below) that show actions and feelings. For example:

- One day, Anya spotted a funny clown standing in the yard.
- The clown handed Anya two tickets.
- They were for the circus that was coming to town.
- The clown was Anya's favorite aunt!

Guided Practice Have students complete the writing frame. Encourage them to use their own words and sentences and to underline the details they add.

Review Invite volunteers to share their narratives with the class. Have listeners use items 1–4 and 7 on the assessment checklist (page 64) to evaluate the effectiveness of other students' stories.

Independent Practice Use the On Your Own activity (page 52) as homework or review. Encourage students to use what they learned in the lesson to complete it. Explain that they can choose a story topic from the Idea Box or use their own idea. Remind them to underline the details they add. You might also invite them to title their stories.

Name _____ Date _____

Clown Surprise

Use the picture to tell a story.

- Focus on your writing purpose.
- Write a good opening sentence.
- Write events in order for a story.
- Use details to show actions and feelings.
- Write your story on another sheet of paper.

Writing Purpose _____

_____

Opening Sentence _____

_____

Sentences in Order _____

_____

_____

_____

_____

_____

_____

On Your Own

Choose a story topic from the Idea Box.
Or think of one of your own.
Complete the page. Use details.
Then, write your story on another sheet of paper.

Idea Box

○ Classmate Asks You to a Sleepover

○ Neighbors Invite You to Go to the Beach

○ Cousin Asks You to Help Build a Snow Fort

○ My Idea: _____

_____

Writing Purpose _____

_____

Opening Sentence _____

_____

Sentences in Order _____

_____

_____

_____

_____

_____

_____

Narrative Writing
Honey Helps

Objectives & Common Core Connections

* Focus on the purpose of narrative writing.
* Develop a good opening sentence.
* Write sentences in sequence.
* Use descriptive words and details to show actions and feelings.
* Write a narrative.

Introduction Provide each student with a copy of the writing frame (page 54). Read the title and first line. Also draw attention to the illustration and read the speech balloons. Tell students that they will write a narrative about the picture. Remind them that a narrative is a story or account of something that is written to entertain the reader.

Model You might say: *You can make up a story based on the picture.* Point out that the first line gives the names of the girl (Joy) and the cat (Honey). Suggest an opening sentence. For example:

* Joy was trying to make a design with bits of colored paper.

Work with students to develop a story. Ask questions, such as: *How does Joy feel about her design? What does Honey do? What do you think will happen next?* For example:

* Honey gets on table and sneezes
* bits of paper go flying
* papers make a new design
* Joy hugs Honey

Coach students in developing complete sentences for the story that elaborate on the events and give the reader more information. Guide them in adding descriptive words and details (underlined below) that show actions and feelings. For example:

* Honey <u>jumped up</u> on the table and <u>let out a great big sneeze</u>.
* Joy's papers <u>flew all over</u>.
* <u>One by one</u>, they <u>landed</u> on the table in <u>a different pattern</u>.
* Joy <u>gave Honey a big hug</u> for the <u>beautiful new design</u>.

Guided Practice Have students complete the writing frame. Encourage them to use their own words and sentences and to underline the details they add.

Review Invite volunteers to share their narratives with the class. Have listeners use items 1–4 and 7 on the assessment checklist (page 64) to evaluate the effectiveness of other students' stories.

Independent Practice Use the On Your Own activity (page 55) as homework or review. Encourage students to use what they learned in the lesson to complete it. Explain that they can choose a helping animal story topic from the Idea Box or use their own idea. Remind them to underline the details they add. You might also invite them to title their stories.

Name _____ Date _____

Honey Helps

How can Honey Cat help Joy
with her design?

- Focus on your writing purpose.
- Write a good opening sentence.
- Write events in order for a story.
- Use details to show actions
  and feelings.
- Write your story on another
  sheet of paper.

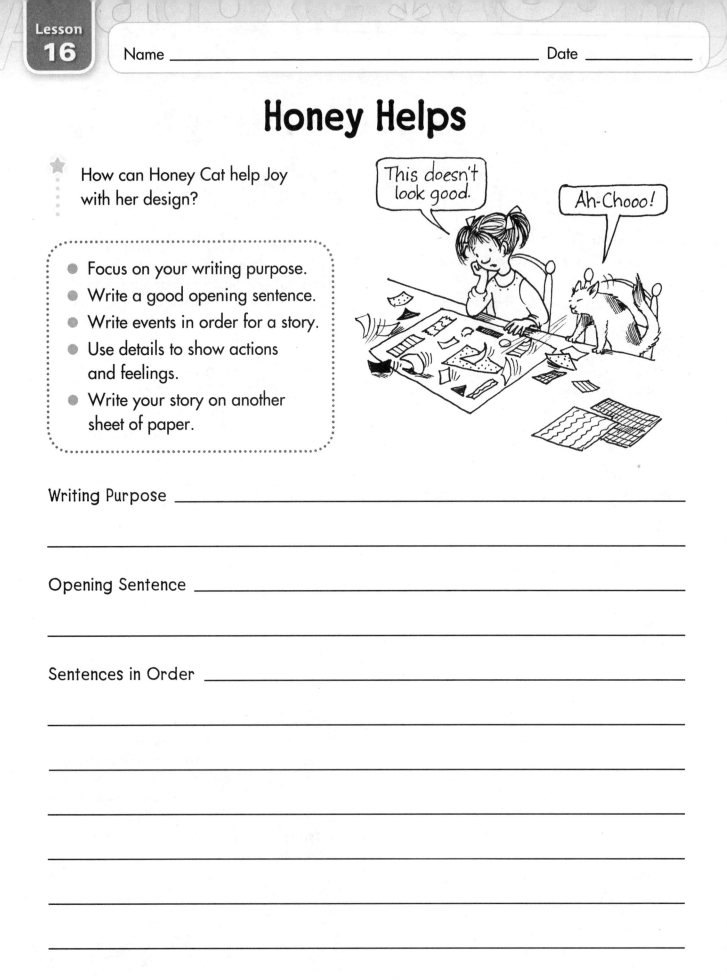

Writing Purpose _____

_____

Opening Sentence _____

_____

Sentences in Order _____

_____

_____

_____

_____

_____

_____

Writing Lessons to Meet the Common Core: Grade 2 © 2013 by Linda Ward Beech, Scholastic Teaching Resources

Name _____ Date _____

On Your Own

Choose a story topic about a helping animal from the Idea Box.
Or think of one of your own.
Complete the page. Use details.
Then, write your story on another sheet of paper.

Idea Box

○ Dog Chases Girl's Runaway Ball

○ Squirrel Knocks Apples to Ground for Family

○ Bird Wakes Up Boy Who Oversleeps

○ My Idea: _____

_____

Writing Purpose _____

_____

Opening Sentence _____

_____

Sentences in Order _____

_____

_____

_____

_____

_____

Narrative Writing
Hat Trouble

Objectives & Common Core Connections

* Focus on the purpose of narrative writing.
* Develop a good opening sentence.
* Write sentences with descriptive words and details.
* Use temporal words to signal event order.
* Write a narrative.

Introduction Provide each student with a copy of the writing frame (page 57). Read the title and first line. Also draw attention to the illustration and read the thought balloon. Tell students that they will write a narrative about the picture. Remind them that a narrative is a story or account of something that is written to entertain the reader. Explain that a narrative can be about something that really happened or it can be make-believe. This story will be make-believe.

Model You might say: *You can make up a story based on the picture.* Tell students that you are going to name the man Ivan. Suggest an opening sentence. For example:

* Ivan had a hat that made him invisible.

Work with students to develop a story. Ask questions, such as: *Where is Ivan? What happens to him when he wears his special hat?* For example:

* goes to a ball game in hat
* other people put their things on his seat
* someone sits on him
* Ivan takes off hat

Coach students in developing complete sentences for the story that elaborate on the events and give the reader more information. Guide them in using descriptive words and details (underlined below) that show actions, thoughts, and feelings. Also include time words, such as *first, next, last, finally*, or *then*, and circle them. Explain that these words help a reader follow the sequence of events. For example:

* Ivan wore his magic hat to a ball game for fun.
* No one knew he was there.
* First, some fans tried to pile their coats onto his seat.
* Then, someone plopped down right on top of him!
* Finally, Ivan decided it would be more fun to take off his hat.

Guided Practice Have students complete the writing frame. Encourage them to use their own words and sentences and to underline the details and circle the time words they add.

Review Invite volunteers to share their narratives with the class. Have listeners use items 1–5 and 7 on the assessment checklist (page 64) to evaluate the effectiveness of other students' stories.

Independent Practice Use the On Your Own activity (page 58) as homework or review. Encourage students to use what they learned in the lesson to complete it. Explain that they can choose a make-believe story topic from the Idea Box or use their own idea. Remind them to underline the details and circle the time words. You might also invite them to title their stories.

Name _____ Date _____

Hat Trouble

How can a hat be a problem?

My hat makes me invisible.

- Focus on your writing purpose.
- Write a good opening sentence.
- Write sentences with details.
- Use time words to show sequence.
- Write your story on another sheet of paper.

Writing Purpose _____

_____

Opening Sentence _____

_____

Sentences in Order _____

_____

_____

_____

_____

_____

_____

Name _____ Date _____

On Your Own

Choose a make-believe story topic from the Idea Box.
Or think of one of your own.
Complete the page. Use details and time words.
Then, write your story on another sheet of paper.

Idea Box

○ Shoes That Make You Run Fast   ○ My Idea: _____

○ A Ring That Makes You Strong   _____

○ A Scarf That Helps You Fly   _____

Writing Purpose _____

_____

Opening Sentence _____

_____

Sentences in Order _____

_____

_____

_____

_____

_____

_____

_____

Narrative Writing
Good Night

Objectives & Common Core Connections

* Focus on the purpose of narrative writing.
* Develop a good opening sentence.
* Write sentences with descriptive words and details.
* Use temporal words to signal event order.
* Provide a sense of closure.
* Write a narrative.

Introduction Provide each student with a copy of the writing frame (page 60). Read the title and first line. Also draw attention to the illustration and speech balloon. Tell students that they will write a narrative about the picture. Review that a narrative is a story or account of something that is written to entertain the reader. Explain that a narrative can be about something that really happened or it can be make-believe.

Model You might say: *You can make up a story based on the picture.* Tell students that you are going to name the boy Finn. Suggest an opening sentence. For example:

* Finn hated bedtime because he could never fall asleep.

Work with students to develop a story. Ask questions, such as: *Is Finn dreaming? Where is he?* For example:

* toy tiger gets Finn out of bed
* they go to jungle
* see birds, insects, plants
* Finn tells family about dream in morning

Coach students in developing complete sentences for the story that elaborate on the events and give the reader more information. Guide them in using descriptive words and details (underlined below) that show actions and feelings. Review the use of time words, such as *first, next, last, finally,* or *then,* and circle them. For example:

* One night Finn's toy tiger pulled him out of bed.
* Then, the tiger led Finn on a hike in a jungle.
* They gazed at lots of colorful and amazing birds, insects, and plants.
* The next morning, Finn shared his dream adventure with his family.

Point out that a story has an ending or conclusion. Give as an example:

* That night Finn couldn't wait for bedtime!

Guided Practice Have students complete the writing frame. Encourage them to use their own words and sentences and to underline the details and circle the time words.

Review Invite volunteers to share their narratives with the class. Have listeners uses items 1–7 on the assessment checklist (page 64) to evaluate the effectiveness of other students' stories.

Independent Practice Use the On Your Own activity (page 61) as homework or review. Encourage students to use what they learned in the lesson to complete it. Explain that they can choose a story topic about a dream from the Idea Box or use their own idea. Remind them to underline the details and circle the time words. You might also invite them to title their stories.

Name _____ Date _____

Good Night

What happens when Finn can't fall asleep?

Come with me.

- Focus on your writing purpose.
- Write a good opening sentence.
- Write sentences with details.
- Use time words to show sequence.
- Write an ending sentence.
- Write your story on another sheet of paper.

Writing Purpose _____

_____

Opening Sentence _____

_____

Sentences in Order _____

_____

_____

_____

_____

Ending Sentence _____

_____

Name _____ Date _____

On Your Own

Idea Box

Choose a story topic for a dream from the Idea Box.
Or think of one of your own.
Complete the page. Use details and time words.
Then, write your story on another sheet of paper.

○ Space
  Trip

○ Underwater
  Exploration

○ Cave
  Visit

○ My Idea:

_____
_____
_____

Writing Purpose _____

_____

Opening Sentence _____

_____

Sentences in Order _____

_____

_____

_____

_____

_____

Ending Sentence _____

_____

Name _____ Date _____

Student Assessment Checklist
Opinion Writing

1. Introduced the topic. .... ☐

2. Focused on the writing purpose. .... ☐

3. Stated an opinion. .... ☐

4. Gave reasons to support the opinion. .... ☐

5. Wrote sentences that include reasons for the opinion. ...... ☐

6. Connected the reasons and opinion with linking words. .... ☐

7. Added a concluding sentence. .... ☐

8. Wrote a paragraph that offers an opinion. .... ☐

More Things to Check

- Capitalized proper nouns. ☐

- Capitalized the first word of sentences. ☐

- Used correct punctuation. ☐

- Spelled words correctly. ☐

- Followed correct paragraph form. ☐

Writing Lessons to Meet the Common Core: Grade 2 © 2013 by Linda Ward Beech, Scholastic Teaching Resources

Student Assessment Checklist
Informative/Explanatory Writing

1. Introduced the topic with a main idea sentence. .... ☐

2. Focused on the writing purpose. .... ☐

3. Used facts to develop the topic. .... ☐

4. Wrote sentences using the facts. .... ☐

5. Listed the materials and steps. .... ☐

6. Wrote a concluding sentence. .... ☐

7. Included a picture. .... ☐

8. Wrote an informative/explanatory paragraph. .... ☐

More Things to Check

● Capitalized proper nouns. ☐

● Capitalized the first word of sentences. ☐

● Used correct punctuation. ☐

● Spelled words correctly. ☐

● Followed correct paragraph form. ☐

Name _____ Date _____

Student Assessment Checklist
Narrative Writing

1. Focused on the writing purpose. .... ☐

2. Wrote a good opening sentence. .... ☐

3. Used descriptive words and details to show actions, thoughts, and feelings. .... ☐

4. Put events in order. .... ☐

5. Used time words to show order of events. .... ☐

6. Wrote an ending sentence. .... ☐

7. Wrote a narrative. .... ☐

More Things to Check

- Capitalized proper nouns. ☐
- Capitalized the first word of sentences. ☐
- Used correct punctuation. ☐
- Spelled words correctly. ☐
- Followed correct paragraph form. ☐

Writing Lessons to Meet the Common Core: Grade 2 © 2013 by Linda Ward Beech, Scholastic Teaching Resources